to:

those who found my bottled tears

and poured them out for me

Prologue:

The people hurting most know the sadness that
takes over and want to keep the darkness away from
others. A smile becomes merely a mask to hide
emotions from the public and laughter is the sound
to disguise the cries from within. I have dealt
with severe depression since childhood. The stigma
behind the word "depression" scared me into
pretending I was immune to the mental illness. I
never wanted people to see me as a fragile soul
who cannot handle pressure or was always
overwhelmed by sadness. I worried people would
view me differently. That was never something I
wanted, so I allowed myself to struggle in silence
for years. I did not come from a rough upbringing;
I have the most loving family. I was reputable in
my hometown for athletics, making it to all-state
games and receiving more all-conference titles
than I can count. I was awarded many honors for my
academics and received scholarships for both my
intellect and sports. I had an image to maintain.

I began thinking I was never enough. I entered
high school with the expectation that I needed
more practice in the gym to become the best
athlete I could be. That I needed to be in the
library longer to become the best student I could
be. I secluded myself to become "the best that I

could be", leading to a lack of social skills and friendships. I never realized how important it is to have someone to lean on. When that realization hit, I substituted my workouts and studying for more minutes with these new friends. I slacked in the gym and library. I found myself faced with the daunting task of preserving grades, a social life, physical shape, and, (if time allotted), sleep. I was intimidated by choice of "what aspect of my life should I sacrifice?" I have known few who can function well with respectable grades, a lively social life, maintained figure and a healthy sleep schedule. I wasn't one of them, I began faltering. I started using alcohol as a crutch. My senior year of high school, I was in full party mode. Spending my last dollar getting ahold of a bottle and feeding my new nicotine addiction. Not my best idea, seeing as alcohol is a depressant and I had already fallen in that dark hole. I had a social life though, people who enjoyed drinking with me. I thought that was what made me happy.

If we rewind a couple months back into those dreaded high school memories, my parents unveiled their plans for divorce halfway through my junior year. My dad moved away, and I wanted to be a role model for my little sisters. I tried to hide my drinking, which, surprise, did not work out well. At that point I no longer attempted to hide it and soon enough my entire family knew. I was following my genetics and becoming yet another alcoholic in the family. Fast forward three days into my senior year; a schoolmate decided to take his life. A friend to many, we held a candlelight vigil to honor our peer. That's when I realized I was a mess. The thoughts that invaded his mind became unbearable, to the point of acting upon them, were the same thoughts invading my mind. Another student took their life in the parking lot 86 days later. I was parked next to my classmate's car

when the gunshot when off. I never even got the
chance to share with his beautiful soul I had
those same demons, we could search for better days
together.

I struggled with anger and grief in the following
months as a domino effect took place and we lost
the lives of too many students. That is how this
book came to be. I wanted to share the thoughts
from the darkest places my mind has traveled to,
as well as the light in the cracks I found while
at the bottom of the depression pit. Darkness has
this way of creeping up on even the strongest of
people, yet there is that glimmer of hope for
everyone. Though I still struggle with my
depression, I wish for people to use this book to
realize they are never alone. For those fortunate
to have not dealt with the darkness at full force,
or not at all, I urge you to use this book as a
reminder to express kindness to all. These
thoughts are shared by far too many and you never
know what kind of battles an individual faces
behind closed doors. The depression pit is a place
many people visit but it doesn't have to be one to
make a shelter of. These are my thoughts from a
heart tired of beating, but nevertheless, still
beats. Happiness is out there, do not let the
darkness overcome and we can put the broken pieces
back together.


I wrote the next passage following the passing of
a classmate. The entirety of my little town was at
a unified low point. We all needed the reminder we
were not struggling alone:


We grew up learning to multiply and divide, to
analyze rhetorical literature and how to write
persuasive papers. We grew up as ignorant robots

set to a fixed eight-hour schedule we were required to attend five days a week, thirty-six weeks a year. We devoted our spare time to additional studies and slept when time allowed. We adjusted our schedules to meet the requirements set by district, collegiate and national standards, not to what we found passion in. We grew up ignored by society, so we set emotional boundaries to keep what was left of our mental capacity safe.

We never learned how to love. Emotional strength was never added to the curriculum, or a course on how to show affection. We were told bullying was frowned upon, yet never taught how not to bully. We were taught how to turn our computers off when we received a hate message, not how to handle the message, nor take it to heart. We were not taught what to say and what not to say, especially when trying to reach out to someone. "I love you" was something said as everyday acknowledgement. We never learned the true value of those three words. Yet, it is still our fault when someone's walls are so destroyed by society's lack of humanity that they resort to the only safe place they know… and we never see them again.

Let us learn how to love someone so deeply that souls connect, and emotional capacities are strengthened. Let us figure out what true self love is and mean it, not just regurgitate it onto a social media platform in attempt to fit in. I want individuals to know that they mean so much to this world and their very being changes how people perceive the galaxies. I want people to love impacting society in such a way they dream of immortality. I want people to crave walking this earth.

If you or anyone you know needs to talk to someone, make the phone call. Use the resources to help find the light.

National Suicide Hotline: 1-800-273-8255

Crisis Text Line: 741741

Immediate Emergency: 911

# table of contents

part I: in my veins

i want to write a poem where the rhythm of each stanza matches the rhythm of your breath.

using your calloused hands as inspiration for the part about missing pieces.

then compare the smile the beach allowed me to the grin you brought me every day.

i will compare the ocean water to the salty tears streaming down my face and proceed to describe why i prefer the oceans acid.

i knew from the beginning the ocean would burn, with you, i didn't.

the use of similes will compare you to a tornado leaving splinters and scars on every surface you touched down on.

the conclusion will leave the reader wondering why the rhythm was so fluid, why the missing pieces were so hard to find, what polluted my tears making them so acidic and why i allowed you to continue to shatter all the shelter i had left.

but it's a cliffhanger

there is no answer

let me be the rope that
pulls your
anchor off the bottom of the sea floor
and allows you to roam free again

let me be the road that
takes you home on the nights
you forget what comfort feels like

let me be the song that you
can't help but smile and sing along to
no matter how awful your day transpired

-safety rope

our infinite forever had a countdown

what does your soul say about me

my demons are cold brewed
masked in sweetener,
they linger in all my favorite cups
drenched in extra caramel.
my demons have tainted each sip
of this plastic encased addiction.
before you there were no demons
lurking in each shot of espresso,
now i can't even escape my demons in
the comfort of my own coffee-
because it reminds me too much of
how you brought me my usual in the mornings

-how to quit an addiction

i need someone to come into my life

and make me want to clean up my act

i will not let you fall,
not your spirits after self-proclaimed failure
or a salted tear on your worst day

i will love you until our immortality deceives us,
you deserve everything the world has to offer
and i will help deliver you to your success

i will wipe my own tears away when you leave,
once i have given every ounce of my soul to you
and you leave for the success i brought you to

-i'll look for your name in the paper

those dreams you have where you are falling
and you feel it in the pit of your stomach

that feeling is present every time i am with you
the irony is that i am falling
but it's not a dream
and i know you will not be there to catch me

bring me sobriety

let me feel drunk in your arms

you will forget how i held your hand the night you
wept

you will forget how bright you smiled the time i
told you i loved you back

you will forget our countless coffee dates, how i
was too stubborn to let you pay

you will forget how much i meant to you while you
hold her hand

and hear her pretend to say i love you

and pay for her coffee

her laugh will replace mine as your favorite music

her smile will become your new screensaver

her body will end up as a newly craved silhouette

you will find how easy it is to keep her because
she is so simple


you'll only remember getting burnt out trying to
keep someone with walls so high you did not want
to attempt climbing over


you will fall in love with settling for easy

because you will forget how happy a complex person
could make you


-the great wall

romeo,

oh romeo

let me drink your poison

lend it to a soul

seeking purpose

she will never be able to move on. she will never be appreciated for her coffee addiction, her love of xxl t shirts and underwear, her hair a constant mess. she will never want to share her true taste in music again because no one will understand the lyrics mean more than just a chorus to her. she will never understand how allowing someone inside her mind caused so much damage. she will never find someone who orders her food exactly how she likes it at every restaurant. she will never be able to return to the places where you both shared the most laughs. she will try to change for the better, only to find her soul deteriorating behind the false front she put up. she will lose sleep thinking about what was wrong with her for someone to move on so fast. she will have trouble deciding outfits in the morning because each shirt holds a memory, she will have to search for the one with the fewest smiles behind it. she will resort to her old ways of despair and constant break downs.

she will never be able to move on; she has changed. her only thought is that she is different now, and no one could love her for it.

-thanks to you

you touch so gently and dedicate
your words to the tender tone i crave.
you loaned me your mind and gave me
insight into a world i never thought possible.
you spoke to me in a way that i
could even see greatness within me.
i returned the favor and dedicated my
every move to showing you how deeply
one could love.
i loaned you my silhouette in the darkest
of nights to show you a galaxy
people find solace in.
i showed you how your sweet words
reiterated could show you your own greatness,
and together we created an infinite forever.

-sweet, sweet forever

your magic

convinced me to

love my flaws,

you left and my

flaws became more

prominent


-home again

your arms began to hold me loosely

then let go sooner

you were removing my shelter

kiss me

with that whiskey grin of yours

let us start something wild

and learn to smile again

i can't relate to the beauty of the moon

the shine of the stars

or the warmth of the sun.

i am like a black hole in the galaxy

too far to be reached,

yet some people admire the complexity


-light years away

until you are out of my mind

i don't know if i can allow

someone else to come and invade

my thoughts


-invaders

im sorry i thought i could fill your cracks, that i could pick up where she left off

im sorry i tried to become her replacement when i knew you would never let her go.

im sorry i ever laughed too deeply or smiled too wide, reminding you of her light chuckle and grin

im sorry you are empty, that your heart strings have been corroded, that you cannot love anyone but her

i wish i could fill that portion of you that she took with her

but i can't, im not her, im sorry.

and,

just like the waves do the shore,

i will always return to you

i wish i played an instrument
so beautifully that it took
everyone's breath away.
each note captured a new heart
and convinced a different soul to be here.
i wish somebody played an instrument
where each note matched mine
and convinced me i had a reason to stay
our melodies matching to create a song
so captivating the world stopped to listen.
the chorus etched into my mind,
the versus stuck on repeat.

each key stroke and each lyric,
a desperate reminder that years of depression
have led to this melody.

-fermata

i want your pure soul

to be rid of the demons

that take away your smile

a vintage soul

could never be loved

in a time where

our eyes are more

focused on a screen

instead of shapes in the clouds


-i see a castle

we were not supposed

to get lost in each other

while still trying to find ourselves


yet here we are


i have fallen for you

and all your demons because

they are mine now


-mine were still scarier

part II: two devils, no angel

Welcome to my dark side.

The part of me trapped by my troubling past.

A past full of depression, death and daunting decisions.

The part of me I could never heal.

It is haunted by these lingering demons whispering delicious sin.

The halls have this hollow laugh that echoes in each corner.

The frames on the walls are memories that have broken a piece of my soul.

The mirrors are all shattered, I hated the reflection I saw so I wrecked them all.

On the ground lay countless bottles I drained in attempt to forget this place.

There is no light here, you are all by yourself.

A projector plays a single movie- more of a documentary really.

It debuts all the doubts and failures I have encountered.

The more enjoyable points have been locked away with no key.

This is my dark side. I am stuck here.

-Get out while you can

I have been told Hell will be

welcoming me,

so I'll give

Hell a reason to

welcome me

with wide arms and a

molten grin.

Remind me that I am alive,

Hurt me as best as you can,

Then maybe I will be numb to the pain.

Give me a single reason to want to be here

When I am alone it's a different story.

My mask begins to drip off my face

As each tear pulls it down.

That bright smile just a play,

The laugh escaping my lips so foreign.


I used to know who I was,

Now I don't recognize my reflection

The devil in her ear begging for sin,

Finally got her to give in.

Even the angel on her shoulder

Dropped her halo.


He was impossible to resist.

The mere scent of temptation,

Was better than anything she had ever tasted

I simply glanced at the bottle,

And it was as if the liquor

Was singing to me.

The delicious tune of coming home.


-90 proof

My sunken eyes

Were my cry for help


-mute

I found my vice,
Something to make my heart burn
And my head fuzzy;
That put a smile on my face
Even if it was only temporary.

That vice was you,
Too bad things change

-your replacement

Even though flying is a dream of mine,

I wouldn't want anyone

To catch me

On the fall down


-selfish thoughts

Feed me lies,

I will drink them like water

The truth is far too vile for me.

Drown me in your famous words,

If not your lies, then give me the strongest proof
you have

Happiness is freighting

I'll wreck your life

I'll make you vulnerable

Why build your hopes up

When you can build your walls up

Could it be,

That my drunk state of mind

Is my true state


-this could be a problem

Sometimes I think to myself
How nice it would be
To not wake up hating myself,
Or maybe not wake up at all

-succumbed to the numbness

Sorry dear,

You can't fix me.


You see, I'm broken

And you can't fix

Something that's broken

If you don't know where

The cracks started

Sometimes I value being alone, no one can hurt you

## Part III: blue heart

i want you to want to be here

i can still teach my sad heart to love the cracks,
it isn't fragile, just bruised and battered


still, everything heals,
even if it never returns to what it once was


i am full of sorrow, yet i have gained wisdom,
now I can recognize another sad heart and teach it
how to repair


with my eyes sunken and soul heavy,
my sad heart will hold those close to me tighter


i take for granted how even battered and bruised
it still beat for me even when i wanted it to quit
like i had


but i didn't want to pass on a sad heart to those
I started to hold so tightly


-i will always have a sad heart

they will always try to

look down on you,

no matter how tall you stand


-closet full of stilettos

attached to nothing

connected to everything

she would rather allow her own feelings to get
hurt than to hurt someone else's

she loves with her entire heart; however her heart
is as stubborn as she is


-words from a devastated father

it is halfway through a laugh
when you don't recognize a genuine tune,
it is surrounded by friends
and convincing yourself
you are just a useless body in the room,
it is the overwhelming feeling of loneliness
when you have a world of people there for you

-tell me again that depression is a joke

just fucking tattoo "i'm fine" on my forehead

it is when i am all alone
and my lonely heart starves for affection,
that the only substance i can provide
is the ample source of dejection.
for my self love is diminished

-positive thoughts

it hurts me to look at someone

with the same pain in their eyes as me

even the most intricate
rose will have its thorns,
leave them there
you don't want to scar her
beauty

why would you let a
single thorn alter how
you view her anyway

-thick thighs and crooked smiles

my last

petal must

have fallen

because I seem

to be a forever

beast


-tainted crown

as the bottle went up,

she slowly loosened her

shackles and let herself free,

liquid freedom from the chains.

people compared her wild smile

to the stars as she told her stories,

but the moon eventually goes

back to sleep and

sends the stars away

-bottle opener

if I treated you the way you deserved,

i can promise you that your heart would fade to
blue


blue claimed my heart,

too bad I don't want to share shades

it is hard to learn to live when

you don't feel alive

you were the drug i craved

every waking moment,

the demon I sought in my sleep,

you were the reason i envied death

yet the sole purpose my chest still rose and fell,

you were the hundred proof whiskey

that went down like water

and the lingering hangover that always followed,

you were the sin I wanted

but could never obtain


-RX

trying to find a shoulder that never comes

i only found a home in the stars

maybe,

one day

someone will admire

the ruins as they are

wipe off the dust,

maybe even

find a way

to admire them


-my autobiography

please

forgive me

for all the pictures

i will take


i often forget

happiness


and sometimes need

to look back

to reminisce


-my hoard of photo albums

we are all waiting to be set free from ourselves,

to become be a somebody


-mental shackles

they asked what happened to my fire

and i say people came and blew it out


they ask why I didn't reignite it

and i say they took my fire when they left


-empty lighter

just hold me,

put your arms around me

and hold me as if the world

depended on it,

because mine does


-super glue

it is not a good idea to love me

part IV: foreign feelings

"my problems are insignificant"

she said

as she sat on the roof

in her oversized hoodie,

just a spec in the entire galaxy


-therapy

oh

but when my heart smiles,

my whole body radiates warmth

and that is what I want you to fall in love with

it is because of you I learned to believe in
myself

do you ever get so lost in a song
you can feel the chorus in your skin
revealing itself as goosebumps,
you close your eyes
finding yourself lost in the sound
and for those couple minutes
everything is okay with the world

-it'll be okay

mama told me to smile more

pops said happiness was flattering

my love,

wait until you experience a sunset while on a
plane

letting your toes sit in the waves while you point
out the few constellations you know

or feeling the warmth of the sun waking up while a
top a mountain,

you will find your soul smiling again

go for the solo trip, prove to yourself you can do
anything

it's okay to let yourself be okay
to let yourself heal

smile a little more and
show off that sweet sweet smile

allow yourself to be happy again

you are a painted canvas

each colored brush stroke an experience,
a defining moment in your life.
your blue hues exposing your pain
and the crimson red your joys in life.

i have never been so in love with lilac before

if you are sharing the stars

with someone who

doesn't think that

your eyes shine brighter,

find someone who

compares your blue hue

to the afternoon sky

home is the sand between my toes with the sun
returning my smile

home is the corner nook of the coffee shop where i
have cried, laughed and shared life's secrets

home is the driver's seat with no destination,
windows down and music blasting

home is in the arms of someone i love, their
embrace warming my soul

home is in each sip of my hot cocoa while all my
friends and i put paint strokes on our canvases


home has never been a place, it's not somewhere I
keep all my belongings

home is that feeling in your heart after a night
of laughter

home is your soul finally smiling

thank you

for looking at a

broken heart

as if it were not

completely shattered

and making it

feel whole again

her free-spirited heart filled the room

everyone fell in love with the way she danced


-modern ballet

one day
it will all make sense,
all the pain and
heartbreak we share.

one day
someone will walk into your life
and be the reason you enjoy
getting out of bed in the morning.

one day
someone will be the reason
you stopped drinking to forget
the skeletons in your closet.

a once so guarded heart
will begin to smile
every time that person is near
and will never fade.

oh, please don't cry

for my tears are for me only.

my heart is merely leaking,

let your heart smile for mine

you are better off without his venom

.

cry as hard as you want

as long as you want

then when you finally dry the streams

be sure to never

cry for the same reason again


-detox

it was the boy with hair dark as a raven
who captured her heart
locked it away and took flight

it was the boy with flaming red hair
that reset her fire
then put out her last embers

it was the boy with chocolate brown hair
that made everything sweet again
before leaving a bitter after taste

it was the girl with platinum blonde hair
that would make herself stronger
before another boy came tearing down her walls
again

allow your soul to cry

heart to break

and mind to rest


for you need never weep

over sorrow more than once,

then you can begin to dance

to the tune of life again

run away with me, let us seek adventure

all she needed

was a little

tequila

to set her soul free

and convince

the world

to love her


-i will drink to that